Sr Mar...

Praying

the Rosary

with Icons

THE CATHOLIC TRUTH SOCIETY
PUBLISHERS TO THE HOLY SEE

CONTENTS

Introduction — 5

THE JOYFUL MYSTERIES — 7
(Monday and Saturday)

    The Annunciation — 8
    The Visitation — 10
    The Birth of Jesus — 12
    The Presentation in the Temple — 14
    Finding Jesus in the Temple — 16

THE MYSTERIES OF LIGHT — 19
(Thursday)

    The Baptism of Jesus — 20
    The Wedding at Cana — 22
    Proclaiming the Kingdom of God — 23
    The Transfiguration — 25
    Instituting the Eucharist — 28

THE SORROWFUL MYSTERIES (Tuesday and Friday)	31
The Agony in the Garden	32
The Crowning with Thorns	34
The Crucifixion	36
The Death of Jesus	38
The Burial	40
THE GLORIOUS MYSTERIES (Wednesday and Friday)	43
The Resurrection	44
The Ascension	46
Pentecost	48
The Assumption of Mary	50
Mary, Queen and Mother	52
Hail Holy Queen	55
Litany of Loreto	55
MARIAN PRAYERS	59
Holy Mother of the Redeemer	59
Under your protection	59
Act of Dedication to Mary	60
Concluding reflection	61

INTRODUCTION

The Word and the Icon. These are the two paths along which we will contemplate the mysteries of the Rosary.

The Word, the first cause, is the 'Word made flesh' in Jesus of Nazareth. This word is written on every page of the life of the Blessed Virgin Mary. These twenty reflections, taken from the four gospels, will illuminate our journey. We will reflect on the most significant episodes of Jesus' life, - the joyous, luminous, sorrowful and glorious episodes. Our journey will culminate in the mystery of his passion, death, and resurrection, and in the Holy Spirit poured out on every believer. We need to listen to the Word in order to accept and understand it.

The icon is a pre-eminent means of contemplation; it is a word written using an alphabet of colours; it is a spring that rises from a long tradition binding east and west together.

These twenty icons will tell the story of the mysteries of the Rosary. They will help to deepen our reflection, and allow us to delve into the gospels in search of hidden treasures. If we look closely and attentively at these icons, they can become a meeting point between us and God, a place of supplication, of healing and of love.

When we contemplate the mysteries of the Rosary, we must never be satisfied with using only our mind or our lips! We must use them both, as well as our eyes and our heart. Only then will we be led into deep and direct contact with the God who can make of each of us an icon of his love.

Jerusalem, 6 January 2010

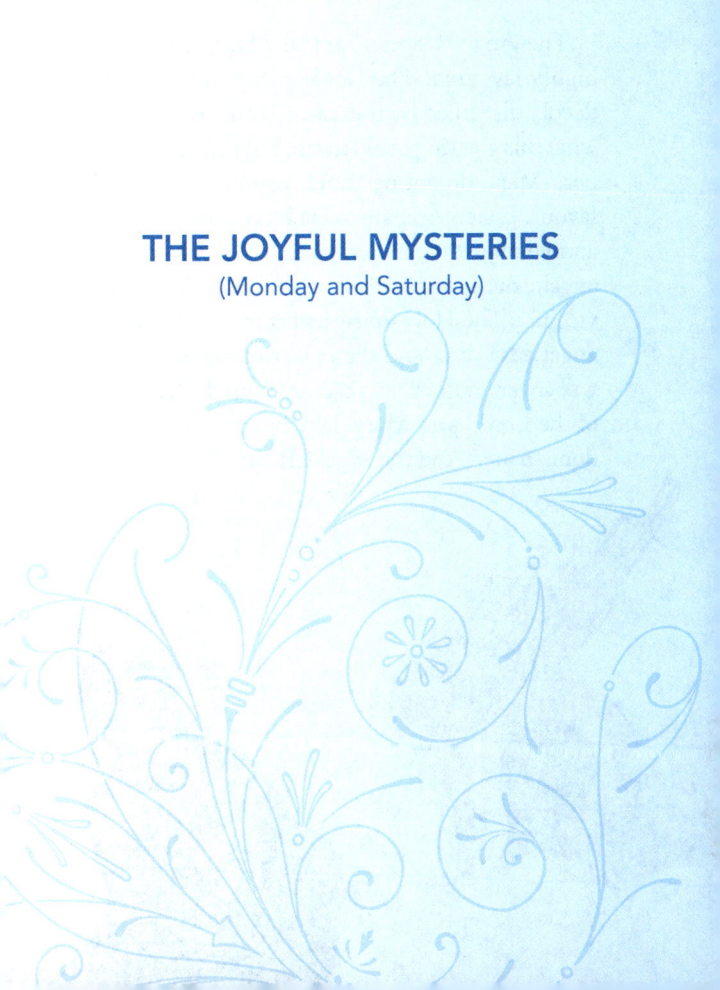

THE JOYFUL MYSTERIES
(Monday and Saturday)

I. THE ANNUNCIATION

The Angel Gabriel said to Mary, 'Rejoice, so highly favoured! The Lord is with you.' She was deeply disturbed by these words and asked herself what this greeting could mean, but the angel said to her, 'Mary, do not be afraid; you have won God's favour. Listen! You are to conceive and bear a son, and you must name him Jesus… Mary said to the angel, 'But how can this come about, since I am a virgin?' 'The Holy Spirit will come upon you' the angel answered 'and the power of the Most High will cover you with its shadow, 'I am the handmaid of the Lord,' said Mary 'let what you have said be done to me.' And the angel left her.

(cf. Lk 1:26-38)

Our Father, 10 Hail Marys, Glory Be

Prayer

Lord Jesus, help me to understand, as Mary did, each time you call me. And give me the grace to answer 'Yes' so that the marvels of God may be seen today.

II. THE VISITATION

Mary set out at that time and went as quickly as she could to a town in the hill country of Judah. She went into Zechariah's house and greeted Elizabeth. Now as soon as Elizabeth heard Mary's greeting, the child leapt in her womb and Elizabeth was filled with the Holy Spirit. She gave a loud cry and said, 'Of all women you are the most blessed, and blessed is the fruit of your womb. For the moment your greeting reached my ears, the child in my womb leapt for joy. Yes, blessed is she who believed that the promise made her by the Lord would be fulfilled.' And Mary said: 'My soul proclaims the greatness of the Lord and my spirit exults in God my saviour.'

(cf. Lk 1:39-47)

Our Father, 10 Hail Marys, Glory Be

Prayer

Lord Jesus, may those I greet, every morning and every day, feel your presence in me so that you may be the light to guide them.

III. THE BIRTH OF JESUS

Now at this time Caesar Augustus issued a decree for a census of the whole world to be taken. This census - the first - took place while Quirinius was governor of Syria, and everyone went to his own town to be registered. So Joseph set out from the town of Nazareth in Galilee and travelled up to Judaea, to the town of David called Bethlehem, since he was of David's House and line, in order to be registered together with Mary, his betrothed, who was with child. While they were there the time came for her to have her child, and she gave birth to a son, her first-born. She wrapped him in swaddling clothes, and laid him in a manger because there was no room for them at the inn.

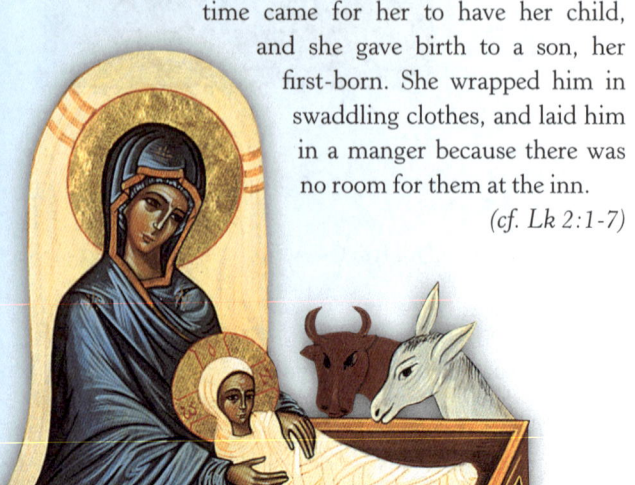

(cf. Lk 2:1-7)

Our Father, 10 Hail Marys, Glory Be

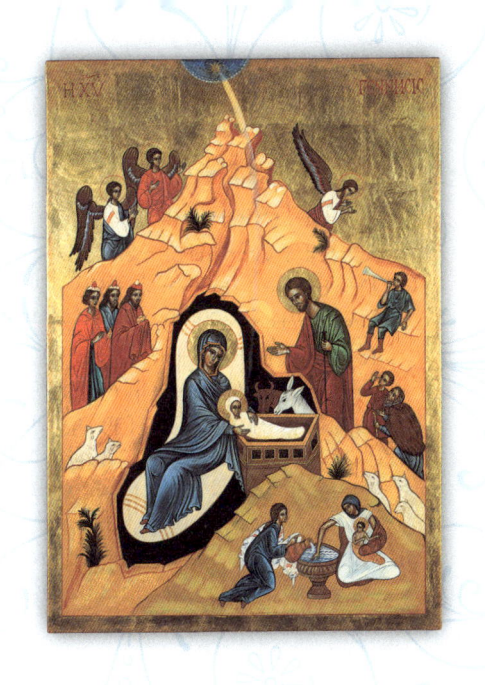

Prayer

Lord Jesus, you wanted to be born during the night in a bare stable. May the morning star rise in my heart and may you be born in the dark and bare places of my being, where I am poor and needy.

IV. THE PRESENTATION IN THE TEMPLE

And when the day came for them to be purified as laid down by the Law of Moses, they took him up to Jerusalem to present him to the Lord - observing what stands written in the Law of the Lord. Simeon took him into his arms and blessed God; and he said: 'Now, Master, you can let your servant go in peace, just as you promised; because my eyes have seen your salvation…' Simeon blessed them and said to Mary his mother, 'You see this child: he is destined for the fall and for the rising of many in Israel, destined to be a sign that is rejected - and a sword will pierce your own soul too - so that the secret thoughts of many may be laid bare'.
(cf. Lk 2:21-28)

Our Father, 10 Hail Marys, Glory Be

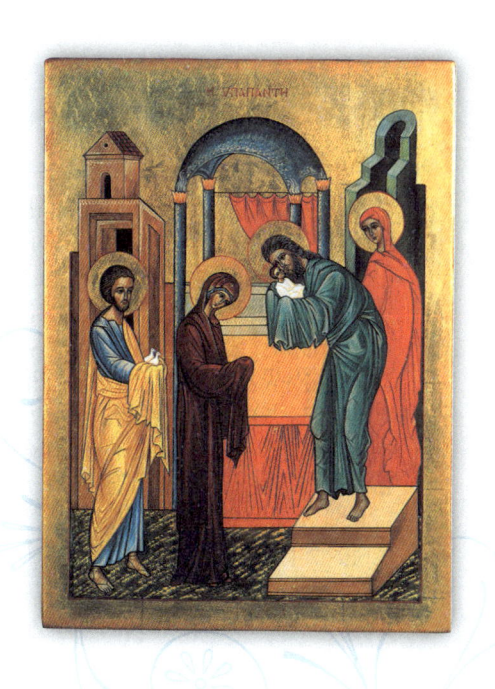

Prayer

Lord Jesus, everything beautiful that I have comes from you, from your love and generosity. I offer it all to you, for your glory and for the salvation of the world.

V. FINDING JESUS IN THE TEMPLE

When he was twelve years old, they went up for the feast as usual. When they were on their way home after the feast, the boy Jesus stayed behind in Jerusalem…They found him in the Temple, sitting among the doctors, listening to them, and asking them questions… His mother said to him, 'My child, why have you done this to us? See how worried your father and I have been, looking for you.' 'Why were you looking for me?' he replied. 'Did you not know that I must be busy with my Father's affairs?' But they did not understand what he meant. He then went down with them and came to Nazareth and lived under their authority. His mother stored up all these things in her heart. And Jesus increased in wisdom, in stature, and in favour with God and men.

(cf. Lk 2:41-52)

Our Father, 10 Hail Marys, Glory Be

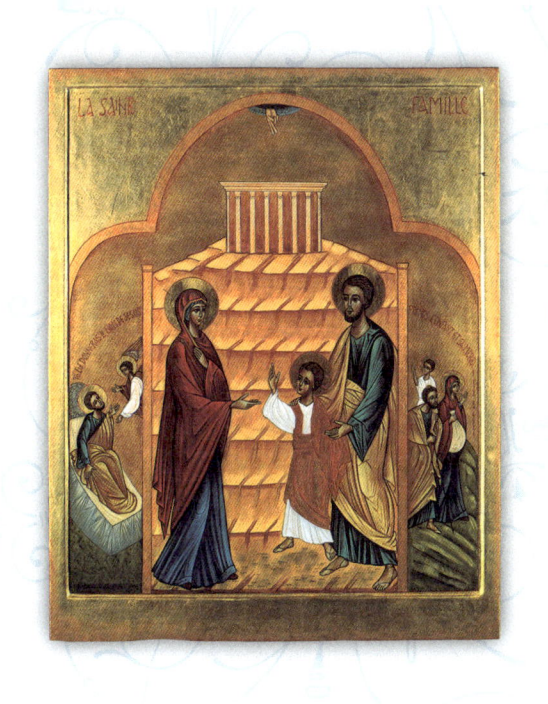

Prayer

O God, give me the grace to know and believe that you are my father. May your tender care surround me and may I never be parted from you.

THE MYSTERIES OF LIGHT
(Thursday)

I. THE BAPTISM OF JESUS

Then Jesus appeared: he came from Galilee to the Jordan to be baptised by John. John tried to dissuade him. 'It is I who need baptism from you' he said 'and yet you come to me!' But Jesus replied, 'Leave it like this for the time being; it is fitting that we should, in this way, do all that righteousness demands'. At this, John gave in to him. As soon as Jesus was baptised he came up from the water, and suddenly the heavens opened and he saw the Spirit of God descending like a dove and coming down on him. And a voice spoke from heaven, 'This is my Son, the Beloved; my favour rests on him'.

(cf. Mt 3:13-17)

*Our Father,
10 Hail Marys,
Glory Be*

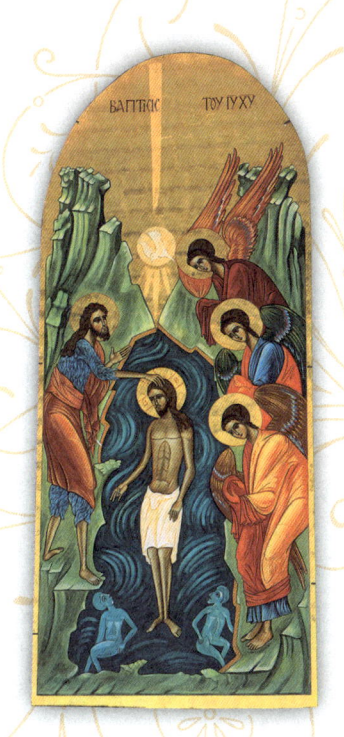

Prayer

Lord Jesus, you wished to descend into the waters of my sin and to transfigure them. Help me to trust you. Help me to tearlessly bury my wrongdoing in the mystery of your baptism and mine, so as to rise from the waters ever more purified.

II. THE WEDDING AT CANA

Three days later there was a wedding at Cana in Galilee. The mother of Jesus was there, and Jesus and his disciples had also been invited. When they ran out of wine ... the mother of Jesus said to him, 'They have no wine'. Jesus said, 'Woman, why turn to me? My hour has not come yet.' His mother said to the servants, 'Do whatever he tells you'. There were six stone water jars standing there ... Jesus said to the servants, 'Fill the jars with water', and they filled them to the brim. 'Draw some out now' he told them 'and take it to the steward.' The steward tasted the water, and it had turned into wine. Having no idea where it came from the steward called the bridegroom and said, 'People generally serve the best wine first, and keep the cheaper sort till the guests have had plenty to drink; but you have kept the best wine till now'.

(cf. Jn 2:1-11)

Our Father, 10 Hail Marys, Glory Be

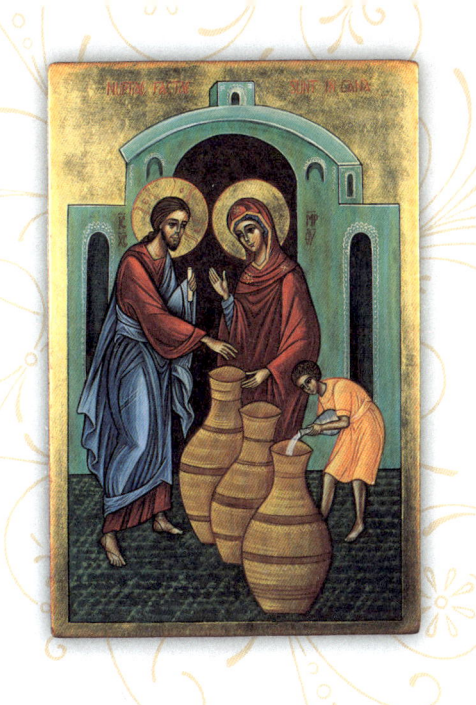

Prayer

Lord Jesus, through the intercession of Mary our mother, change my water into wine, for the good of those who surround me, so that I may be able to continue to celebrate my union with you.

III. PROCLAIMING THE KINGDOM OF GOD

After John had been arrested, Jesus went into Galilee. There he proclaimed the Good News from God. 'The time has come' he said 'and the kingdom of God is close at hand. Repent, and believe the Good News.'

(cf. Mk 1:14-15)

Our Father, 10 Hail Marys, Glory Be

Prayer

Lord Jesus, I do not know how to speak or how to teach. You can do all things; enter the events of my everyday life. Transform my life into an example of your care and love, so that I may become what you want me to be: the light of the world.

IV. THE TRANSFIGURATION

Jesus took with him Peter and John and James and went up the mountain to pray. As he prayed, the aspect of his face was changed and his clothing became brilliant as lightning. Suddenly there were two men there talking to him; they were Moses and Elijah appearing in glory, and they were speaking of his passing which he was to accomplish in Jerusalem...Peter said to Jesus, 'Master, it is wonderful for us to be here; so let us make three tents, one for you, one for Moses and one for Elijah'. He did not know what he was saying. As he spoke, a cloud came and covered them with shadow; and when they went into the cloud the disciples were afraid. And a voice came from the cloud saying, 'This is my Son, the Chosen One. Listen to him.'

(cf. Lk 9:28-36)

*Our Father,
10 Hail Marys,
Glory Be*

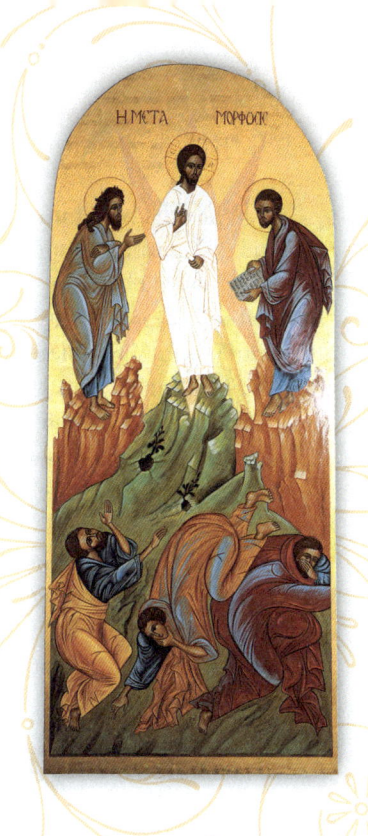

Prayer

Lord Jesus, you destroy nothing and transfigure everything. Transfigure my sufferings, pains, shortcomings and weaknesses, so that they may all lead me closer to you.

V. INSTITUTING THE EUCHARIST

When the hour came he took his place at table, and the apostles with him. And he said to them, 'I have longed to eat this Passover with you before I suffer; because, I tell you, I shall not eat it again until it is fulfilled in the kingdom of God'.

Then, taking a cup, he gave thanks and said, 'Take this and share it among you, because from now on, I tell you, I shall not drink wine until the kingdom of God comes'. Then he took some bread, and when he had given thanks, broke it and gave it to them, saying, 'This is my body which will be given for you; do this as a memorial of me'. He did the same with the cup after supper, and said, 'This cup is the new covenant in my blood which will be poured out for you.'

(cf. Lk 22:14-20)

Our Father, 10 Hail Marys, Glory Be

Prayer

Lord Jesus, you want to make of me an altar and a tabernacle. Help me to unite my body and blood to your body and blood consecrated on the altar each day. May I become a true resting place and tabernacle for your presence.

THE SORROWFUL MYSTERIES
(Tuesday and Friday)

I. THE AGONY IN THE GARDEN

He made his way as usual to the Mount of Olives, with the disciples following. He said to them, 'Pray not to be put to the test'. Then he withdrew from them, about a stone's throw away, and knelt down and prayed. 'Father,' he said 'if you are willing, take this cup away from me. Nevertheless, let your will be done, not mine.' Then an angel appeared to him, coming from heaven to give him strength. In his anguish he prayed even more earnestly, and his sweat fell to the ground like great drops of blood. He went to the disciples and found them sleeping for sheer grief. 'Why are you asleep?' he said to them. 'Get up and pray not to be put to the test.'

(cf. Lk 22:39-46)

Our Father, 10 Hail Marys, Glory Be

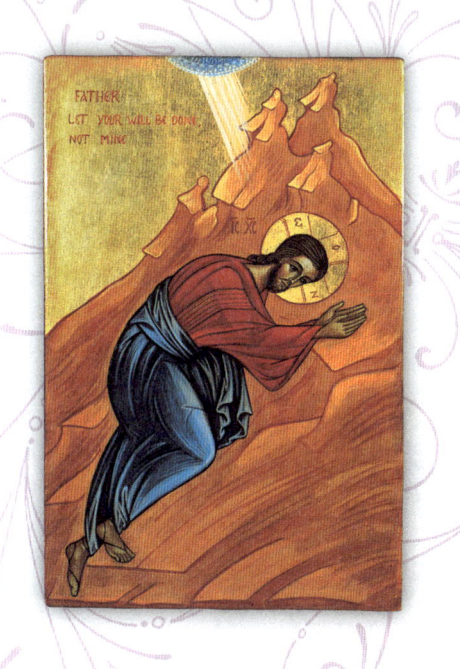

Prayer

Lord Jesus, when I feel crushed under the weight of a trial, or a hard and difficult experience, grant that I may have the grace to unite my prayer with yours and have the strength to say with you, 'Father, let your will be done, not mine.'

II. THE CROWNING WITH THORNS

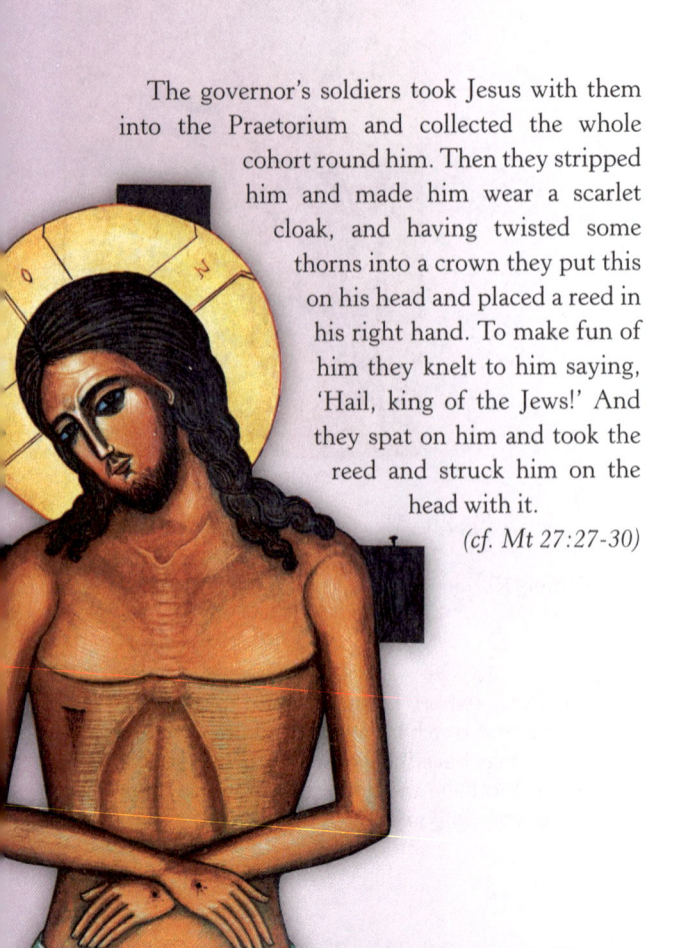

The governor's soldiers took Jesus with them into the Praetorium and collected the whole cohort round him. Then they stripped him and made him wear a scarlet cloak, and having twisted some thorns into a crown they put this on his head and placed a reed in his right hand. To make fun of him they knelt to him saying, 'Hail, king of the Jews!' And they spat on him and took the reed and struck him on the head with it.

(cf. Mt 27:27-30)

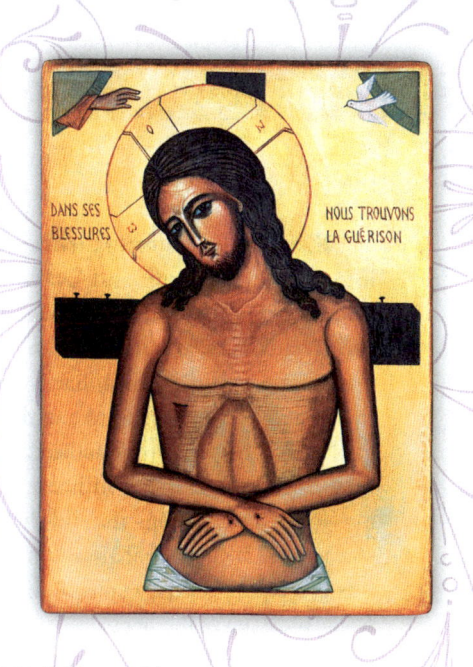

Our Father, 10 Hail Marys, Glory Be

Prayer

O God, you told Adam, 'The earth will yield brambles and thistles' and now Jesus, in his passion allows himself to be crowned with thorns and brambles, never opening his mouth. Give me the grace to bear silently with all the things that hurt, wound and humiliate me, so that one day, you may transform them into a glorious crown.

III. THE CRUCIFIXION

When they had finished making fun of him, they led him away to crucify him. On their way out, they came across a man from Cyrene, Simon by name, and enlisted him to carry his cross. When they had reached a place called Golgotha, that is, the place of the skull, they gave him wine to drink mixed with gall, which he tasted but refused to drink. When they had finished crucifying him they shared out his clothing by casting lots, and then sat down and stayed there keeping guard over him. Above his head was placed the charge against him; it read: 'This is Jesus, the King of the Jews'.

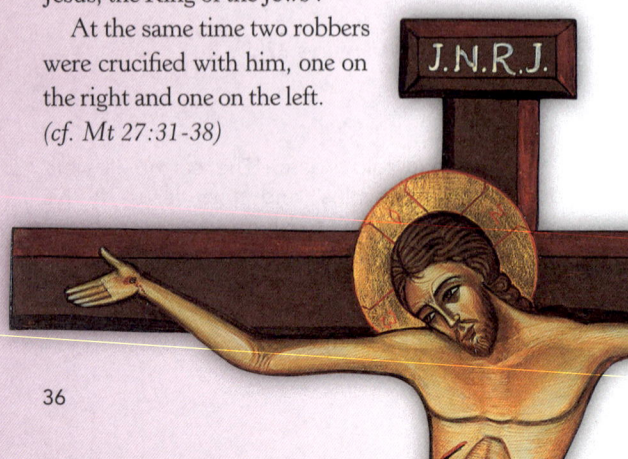

At the same time two robbers were crucified with him, one on the right and one on the left.
(cf. Mt 27:31-38)

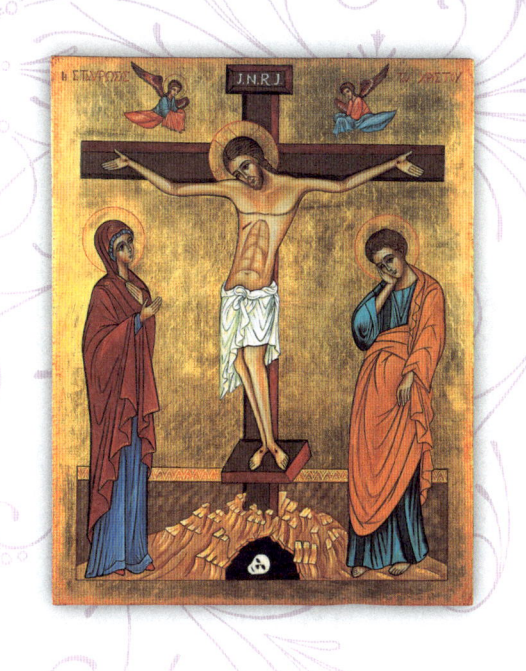

Our Father, 10 Hail Marys, Glory Be

Prayer

Lord Jesus, you carried our sins onto the cross, you are the Lamb of God who takes away the sins of the world. Give me the grace to hand my sins over to you and to unite my crosses, both large and small, 'good' and 'bad', with yours.

IV. THE DEATH OF JESUS

One of the criminals hanging there abused him. 'Are you not the Christ?' he said. 'Save yourself and us as well.' But the other spoke up and rebuked him. 'Have you no fear of God at all?' he said. 'You got the same sentence as he did, but in our case we deserved it: we are paying for what we did. But this man has done nothing wrong. Jesus,' he said 'remember me when you come into your kingdom.' 'Indeed, I promise you,' he replied 'today you will be with me in paradise.' It was now about the sixth hour and, with the sun eclipsed, a darkness came over the whole land until the ninth hour. The veil of the Temple was torn right down the middle; and when Jesus had cried out in a loud voice, he said, 'Father, into your hands I commit my spirit.' With these words he breathed his last.

(cf. Lk 23:39- 46)

Our Father, 10 Hail Marys, Glory Be

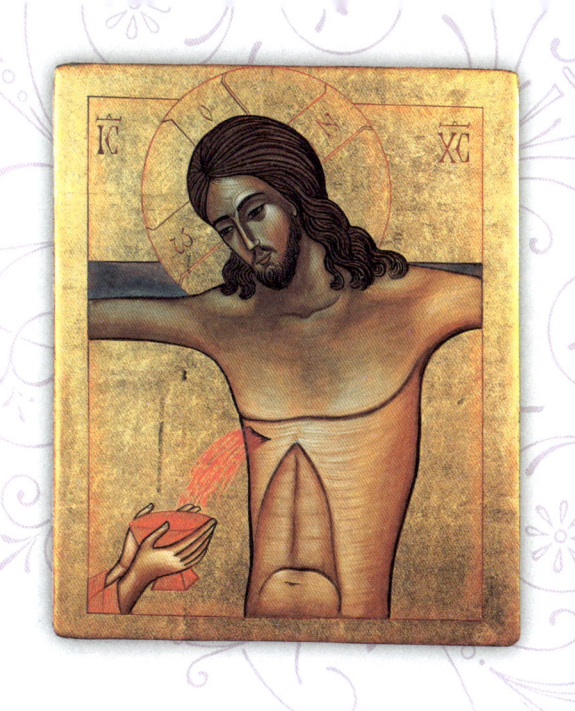

Prayer

Lord Jesus, you told the good thief 'Today you will be with me in paradise'. So you have shown that death is not the end, but only a new birth. Make me a witness to this hope.

V. THE BURIAL

Then a member of the council arrived, an upright and virtuous man named Joseph. He had not consented to what the others had planned and carried out. He came from Arimathaea, a Jewish town, and he lived in the hope of seeing the kingdom of God. This man went to Pilate and asked for the body of Jesus. He then took it down, wrapped it in a shroud and put him in a tomb which was hewn in stone in which no one had yet been laid. It was Preparation Day and the sabbath was imminent. Meanwhile the women who had come from Galilee with Jesus were following behind. They took note of the tomb and of the position of the body.

(cf. Lk 23:50-56)

Our Father, 10 Hail Marys, Glory Be

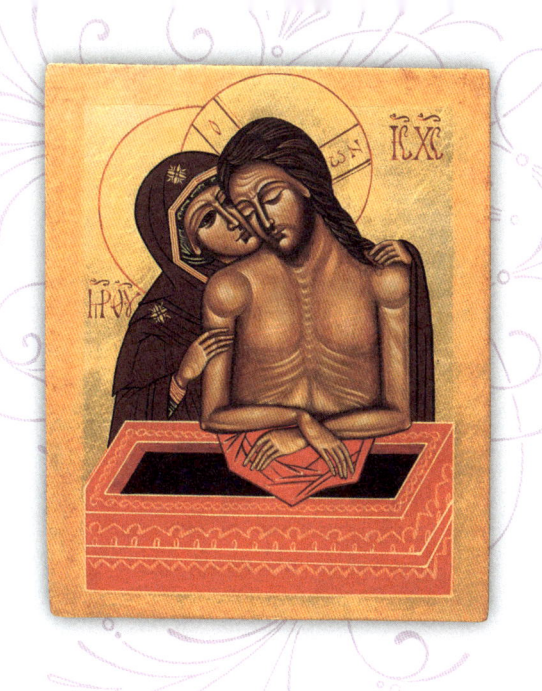

Prayer

Lord Jesus, you gave Mary to be our Mother. Help me to wait at the foot of the cross with her, in uprightness and faith, for my own resurrection and that of all my dear departed family and friends.

THE GLORIOUS MYSTERIES
(Wednesday and Sunday)

I. THE RESURRECTION

After the sabbath, and towards dawn on the first day of the week, Mary of Magdala and the other Mary went to visit the sepulchre. And all at once there was a violent earthquake, for the angel of the Lord, descending from heaven, came and rolled away the stone and sat on it. His face was like lightning, his robe white as snow. The guards were so shaken, so frightened of him, that they were like dead men. But the angel said to the women, 'There is no need for you to be afraid. I know you are looking for Jesus, who was crucified. He is not here, for he has risen, as he said he would. Come and see the place where he lay.
(cf. Mt 28:1-8)

Our Father, 10 Hail Marys, Glory Be

Prayer

Lord Jesus, you descended into hell to announce complete freedom for all your creation. You returned from the kingdom of the dead to tell us, 'I am the living One and I will be with you until the end of time.' May this assurance help me to experience the joy of your resurrection.

II. THE ASCENSION

Jesus said to his disciples, 'You will receive power when the Holy Spirit comes on you, and then you will be my witnesses not only in Jerusalem but throughout Judaea and Samaria, and indeed to the ends of the earth'. As he said this he was lifted up while they looked on, and a cloud took him from their sight. ... So from the Mount of Olives, as it is called, they went back to Jerusalem, a short distance away, no more than a sabbath walk; and when they reached the city they went to the upper room where they were staying; there were Peter and John, James and Andrew, Philip and Thomas, Bartholomew and Matthew, James son of Alphaeus and Simon the Zealot, and Jude son of James. All these joined in continuous prayer, together with several women, including Mary the mother of Jesus, and with his brothers.

(cf. Ac 1:6-14)

Our Father, 10 Hail Marys, Glory Be

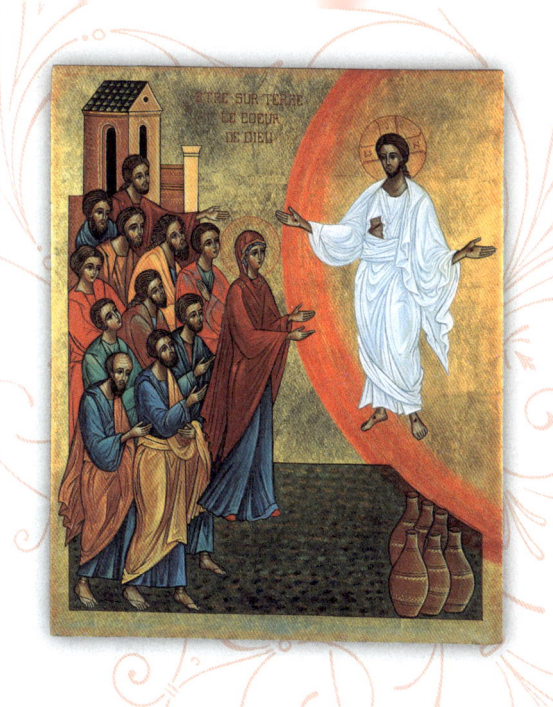

Prayer

Lord Jesus, you ascended into heaven before the very eyes of men, but in your mysterious love you dwell in our hearts. You who now sit at the right hand of the Father, make my heart a fitting place for you to dwell in.

III. PENTECOST

When Pentecost day came round, they had all met in one room, when suddenly they heard what sounded like a powerful wind from heaven, the noise of which filled the entire house in which they were sitting; and something appeared to them that seemed like tongues of fire; these separated and came to rest on the head of each of them. They were all filled with the Holy Spirit, and began to speak foreign languages as the Spirit gave them the gift of speech.

(cf. Ac 2:1-4)

Our Father, 10 Hail Marys, Glory Be

Prayer
    Lord Jesus, send me your Holy Spirit, that it may guide and inspire me, especially when making difficult choices. Above all, teach me to love as you love.

IV. THE ASSUMPTION OF MARY

Now a great sign appeared in heaven: a woman, adorned with the sun, standing on the moon, and with the twelve stars on her head for a crown. She was pregnant, and in labour, crying aloud in the pangs of childbirth. Then a second sign appeared in the sky, a huge red dragon which had seven heads and ten horns, and each of the seven heads crowned with a coronet. Its tail dragged a third of the stars from the sky and dropped them to the earth, and the dragon stopped in front of the woman as she was having the child, so that he could eat it as soon as it was born from its mother. The woman brought a male child into the world, the son who was to rule all the nations with an iron sceptre, and the child was taken straight up to God and to his throne.

(cf. Rv 12:1-6)

Our Father, 10 Hail Marys, Glory Be

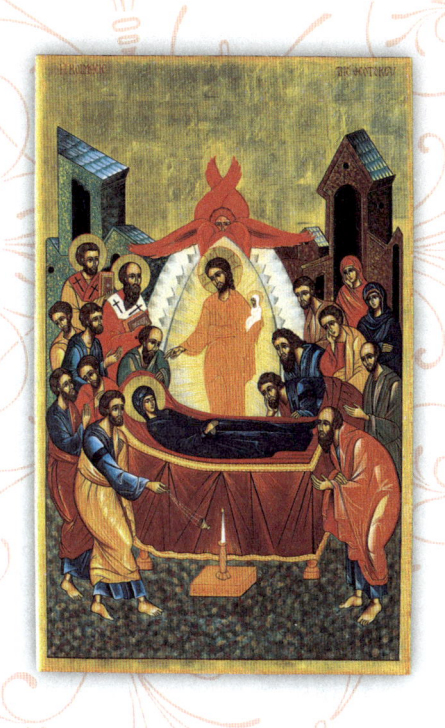

Prayer

O Virgin Mary, your assumption into heaven prefigures that of every man. Intercede with your Son that he may help me to grow in goodness each day, and to raise my heart towards the Father.

V. MARY, QUEEN AND MOTHER

And Mary said: 'My soul proclaims the greatness of the Lord and my spirit exults in God my saviour; because he has looked upon his lowly handmaid. Yes, from this day forward all generations will call me blessed, for the Almighty has done great things for me. Holy is his name. ... He has shown the power of his arm, he has routed the proud of heart. He has pulled down princes from their thrones and exalted the lowly. The hungry he has filled with good things, the rich sent empty away.

(Lk 1:46-55)

*Our Father,
10 Hail Marys,
Glory Be*

Prayer

Mary, you are my hope and my joy. All the desires of humanity were fulfilled in you. You are compassionate towards all, towards the poorest and those most in need. Now that nothing can limit your love, we pray that you remember us always.

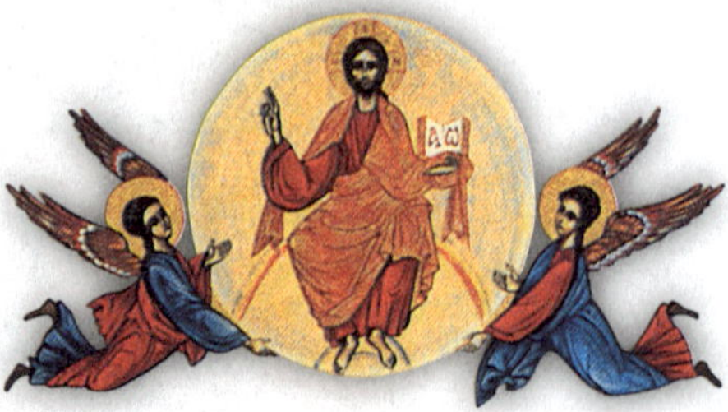

Hail Holy Queen

Hail, holy Queen, Mother of Mercy, hail our life, our sweetness and our hope. To thee do we cry, poor banished children of Eve; to thee do we send up our sighs, mourning and weeping in this valley of tears. Turn then, most gracious advocate, thine eyes of mercy towards us; and after this our exile, show unto us the blessed fruit of thy womb, Jesus.
O clement, O loving, O sweet Virgin Mary.

Litany of Loreto

Lord, have mercy	*Lord, have mercy*
Christ, have mercy	*Christ, have mercy*
Lord, have mercy	*Lord, have mercy*
Christ, hear us	*Christ, hear us*
Christ, graciously hear us	*Christ, graciously hear us*
God, the Father of heaven	*Have mercy on us*
God the Son, Redeemer of the world	*(repeat)*
God, the Holy Spirit	*(repeat)*
Holy Trinity, One God	*(repeat)*

Holy Mary	*pray for us*
Holy Mother of God	*(repeat)*
Holy Virgin of virgins	
Mother of Christ	
Mother of divine grace	
Mother most pure	
Mother most chaste	
Mother inviolate	
Mother undefiled	
Mother most amiable	
Mother most admirable	
Mother of good counsel	
Mother of our Creator	
Mother of our Saviour	
Virgin most prudent	
Virgin most venerable	
Virgin most renowned	
Virgin most powerful	
Virgin most merciful	
Virgin most faithful	
Mirror of justice	
Seat of wisdom	
Cause of our joy	
Spiritual vessel	
Vessel of honour	
Singular vessel of devotion	
Mystical rose	
Tower of David	
Tower of ivory	
House of gold	
Ark of the covenant	
Gate of Heaven	
Morning star	

Health of the sick
Refuge of sinners
Comforter of the afflicted
Help of Christians
Queen of Angels
Queen of Patriarchs
Queen of Prophets
Queen of Apostles
Queen of Martyrs
Queen of Confessors
Queen of Virgins
Queen of all Saints
Queen conceived without Original Sin
Queen assumed into Heaven
Queen of the most holy rosary
Queen of the family
Queen of Peace

Lamb of God, who take away the sins of the world
spare us Lord

Lamb of God, who take away the sins of the world
graciously hear us, O Lord

Lamb of God, who take away the sins of the world
have mercy on us

Pray for us, O holy Mother of God
That we may be made worthy of the promises of Christ

Prayer

O God, whose only-begotten Son, by his life, death and resurrection, has purchased for us the rewards of eternal life; grant, we beseech you, that meditating on these Mysteries of the most holy Rosary of the Blessed Virgin Mary, we may both imitate what they contain, and obtain what they promise, through the same Christ our Lord.

Amen.

MARIAN PRAYERS

Loving Mother of the Redeemer

O Holy Mother of the Redeemer,
Gate of heaven, star of the sea,
Assist your people who have fallen,
as we strive to rise again.
To the wonderment of nature,
You bore your Creator,
Yet remained a virgin as before.
You who received Gabriel's joyful greeting,
Have pity on us poor sinners.

Amen.

Under your protection

We fly to thy protection,
O holy Mother of God,
despise not our petitions in our necessities,
but deliver us always from all dangers,
O glorious and blessed Virgin.

Amen.

Act of Dedication to Mary

Receive me, O mother Mary,
teacher and queen,
among those you love, feed, guide and sanctify
in the school of Jesus Christ the divine Teacher.

You see in the mind of God the children he calls,
and you prepare intercession, graces, light and
special comfort for them.
My teacher, Jesus Christ, gave himself wholly to you,
from his incarnation to his ascension;
this for me is an infallible example and gift:
I too, give myself completely into your hands.

Procure for me the grace to know,
imitate and love the divine master
who is the way, the truth and the life.
You bring me, an unworthy sinner, before Jesus.
I cannot enter his school save by your intercession.

Enlighten my mind,
strengthen my will,
sanctify my heart that I may profit of so much mercy,
so that I may say at my ending:
'It is not I who live, but Christ who lives in me'.

Amen.

CONCLUDING REFLECTION

Our holy mother thrice experienced motherhood:

- The first was when she, the Immaculate Conception, by grace, conceived in her soul the son of God, so that he might be her first and only child.
- The second was when, thanks to the Holy Spirit, she generated the Son of God and carried him in her body.
- The third was when our Lord, dying on the cross, wanted to draw his risen life, firstly from the heart of his own mother, by the strength of her faith and compassionate love. In this way he gave life to the entire mystical body of Christ thanks to the Virgin Mary who was its heart - as well as giving graces to those who wish to love him. Thus, he left his Church after his death, a stronger and more excellent life than the one he had given up while living.

What did the Son, out of pure grace, give to the soul of the Virgin in her first motherhood? The Holy Spirit - as author and fountain of grace. It was also the Holy Spirit that made his birth in time possible: *concepit de Spiritu Sancto*.

It was also the Holy Spirit that, in her third motherhood, made it possible for the Son, dying on the cross, to take up his life again.

This was thanks to the heart of the Virgin that was filled with a strong and powerful love for her Son, a love greater than any she had yet experienced.

Father Joseph of Tremblay, 17th Century
Founder of the Benedictine Congregation of Our Lady of Calvary

A New Rosary Book

Including the Mysteries of Light

This booklet is intended for those coming to the Rosary for the first time, and those who are already familiar with it. It explains everything about the Rosary, how the 'mysteries' are prayed, Rosary beads used, and various customs attached to the prayer. It also explains the practical steps of saying the Rosary, with helpful instructions and all the various prayers that are used. The booklet contains scripture passages to aid contemplation of each of the Mysteries, including the recently introduced 'Mysteries of Light' (or 'Luminous Mysteries').

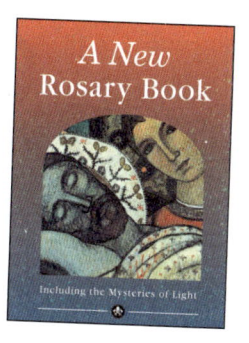

This new Rosary book responds to John Paul II's call to rediscover the Rosary. The inspired recommendations of his Apostolic Letter *Rosarium Virginis Mariae* (2002) are woven throughout. A final section considers why it is important to rediscover the Rosary.

CTS Code: D 659
ISBN: 978 1 86082 181 3

A world of Catholic reading at your fingertips ...

CTS

... now online
Browse 500 titles at
www.cts-online.org.uk

Catholic Faith, Life, and Truth for all   CTS